POWDER POWDER

A SNOWBOARDING BOOK FOR KIDS

WRITTEN AND
ILLUSTRATED BY

M.C. HENRY

@mchenrybooks

Powder Power

This book belongs to:

_____

Powder Power

POWDER POWER

A SNOWBOARDING BOOK FOR KIDS

BY M.C. HENRY

Powder Power

Dedicated to my dad Michael for encouraging me to draw,
and to my grandpa John for teaching me how to ski.
Also dedicated to all who supported me
and helped make this book possible.

 **@mchenrybooks**

Powder Power

Powder Power

Make sure you have all your gear. Each piece serves a special purpose.

Snow goggles
-Blocks snow, wind, and snow glare

Helmet
-Helps protect your brain and keeps you warm

Snow Bibs
-Fully waterproof to stay dry all day

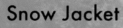

Snow Jacket
-Designed to be waterproof and weatherproof

Snowboard
-Can't go snowboarding without this

Snow Gloves
-Keeps your hands warm and dry

Snowboard Boots
-Specialized to attach with most snowboards perfectly

Powder Power

Some tools are optional, yet recommended.

Face Protection
-*Essential in blizzard conditions*
-*Protects face from snow and ice*
-*A simple scarf or balaclava can be used to cover exposed skin*

Compact Shovel
-*The perfect tool for sculpting jumps and shaping features*
-*Can be utilized for many uses*

Snowboard Leash

-*Anchors your board to your body*
-*Helps protect other riders*

Communication Tools

-*Radio transceivers work well in isolated areas*
-*A simple whistle can be a valuable tool when all else fails*

Stomp Pad
-*Attaches to the snowboard for added traction*
-*Greatly enhances maneuverability when rear foot is unstrapped*

Powder Power

Warming up on flat ground is a good idea, especially for beginners.

Powder Power

Powder Power

No need to rush with views like this.

Powder Power

When both feet are attached, standing up is harder than it looks.

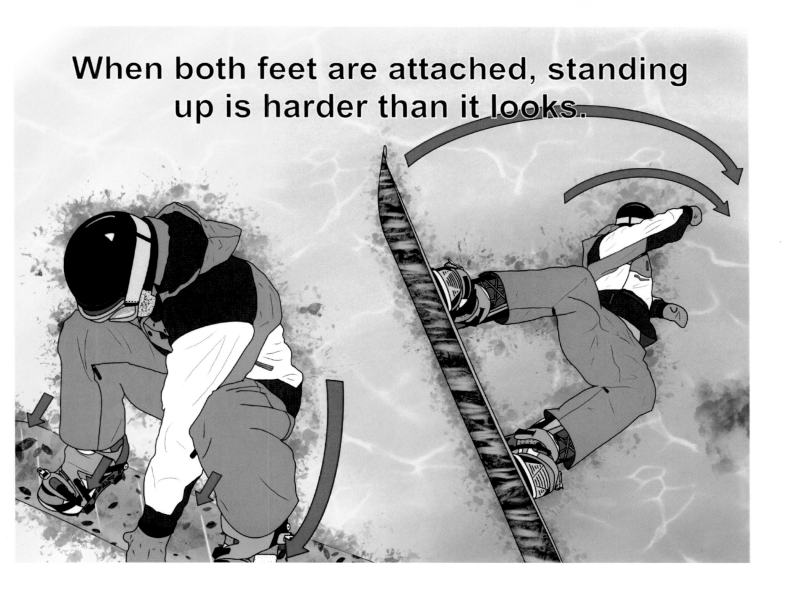

Powder Power

Leaning back looks cool, but makes your board more difficult to control.

Powder Power

Instead of leaning back embrace a forward leaning stance.

Powder Power

A downhill leaning stance allows you to turn and slow down on steep hills.

Powder Power

Powder Power

Powder Power

Powder Power

Not all snowboards behave the same way.

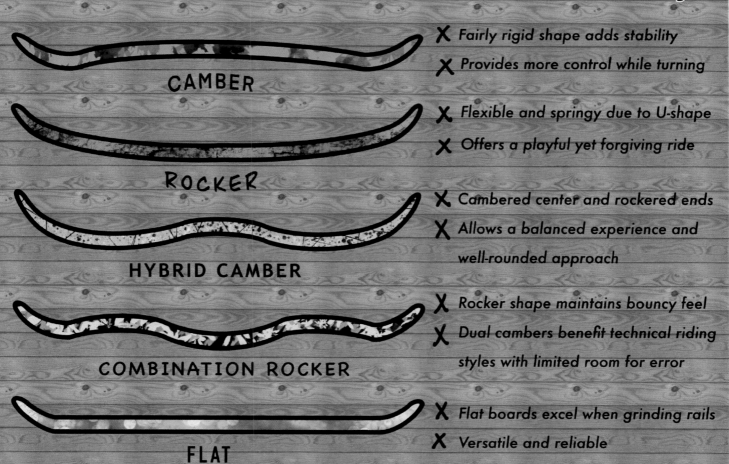

CAMBER
- X Fairly rigid shape adds stability
- X Provides more control while turning

ROCKER
- X Flexible and springy due to U-shape
- X Offers a playful yet forgiving ride

HYBRID CAMBER
- X Cambered center and rockered ends
- X Allows a balanced experience and well-rounded approach

COMBINATION ROCKER
- X Rocker shape maintains bouncy feel
- X Dual cambers benefit technical riding styles with limited room for error

FLAT
- X Flat boards excel when grinding rails
- X Versatile and reliable

Powder Power

Part of learning how to snowboard is learning how to fall safely.

Powder Power

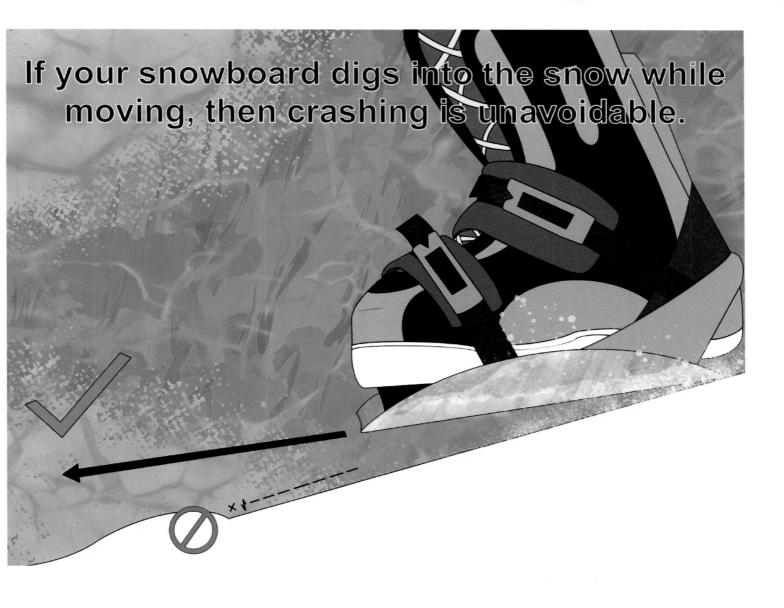

Powder Power

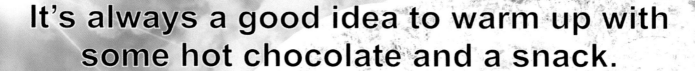

It's always a good idea to warm up with some hot chocolate and a snack.

Powder Power

Powder Power

Powder Power

M.C. Henry was born and raised in the Pacific Northwest, and has over two decades of skiing and snowboarding experience under his belt.

While he enjoys illustrating, M.C. Henry's true passion is writing. He has published two previous titles under various pen names. His favorite genres to explore are science fiction, comedy, are horror.

One goal of his is to snowboard Japan's hidden backcountry. When there's no snow around M.C. Henry likes to explore nature, hang out with friends, and enjoy new foods.

For more information and to stay updated on future titles, follow @mchenrybooks on Twitter. Thank you for your support, and have fun out there shredding the snow.

Powder Power

Made in the USA
Las Vegas, NV
22 December 2020

14523551R00031